URBAN SURFING

Poems by Eveline Marius
Photographs by Alan Denney

This book is about an unspoken conversation sustained throughout the 1980s between a poet and a photographer. A conversation embarked on some thirty years later, recalling community life as it then was in Hackney, an inner London borough. At the end they paused, momentarily, for yet another cup of tea and a 'roll up', pleased with having journeyed down memory lane. The gem you find in your hands is the end product of that conversation.

Why did it take them so long? Simple. What wordsmith Eveline Marius and photographer Alan Denney probably did in the '80s, as social workers enjoying a cheeky drag on a roll-up during a break from office work, was let off steam about their out-of-touch managers and reflect on their unsparing casework. For sure, at the time they could not foresee that one day they would join forces to see these poems and photographs published in this beautifully crafted book.

Eveline's poems, penned throughout the '80s, and Alan's pictures, snapped during the first half of that decade, capture Hackney's working-class poverty, poor housing, racism, and police harassment. Or just plain life. They speak to us about community, that malleable concept which serves to give meaning to Hackney's urban surfers going about their everyday routines of work, leisure, shopping, or just 'hanging out'.

Eveline, born in 1955 in French Guyana, lived in St Lucia for six years before moving to England in 1965. Inspired at school to listen to Mozart, Tchaikovsky and other classical composers, and to study the poetry of Lord Byron, Samuel Taylor Coleridge and Robert Burns, Eveline began to 'play with words'. In 1982 she penned 'Down in the Ghetto', about the ennui engendered by daily 'going down to the same old front line' (then on Sandringham Road). In the same year Hackney's Centerprise community bookshop published some of her poems in *As Good as We Can Make It*. And in 1988 Sheba Press, a Hackney-based feminist cooperative, published three of her poems in *Charting the Journey: Writings by Black and Third World Women*. These, among others penned on scraps of paper or into an exercise book during the '80s and '90s, make their appearance in this collection.

Alan, born in 1952, was brought up in Gillingham, Kent. It was a working-class town then hinged round its naval dockyard. In 1974 he moved to Hackney where he has lived ever since. He began photographing the borough in all its ethnic diversity, taking his inspiration from photographers whose radical politics were shaped by the student and working-class struggles of the late '60s. His photography came to public attention in 2008 when, having put much of his work online, it attracted 'millions of views' according to an interview he gave to *Hackney Magazine* in 2017.

What was Hackney like in the 1980s? It depended on one's 'manor'. Dalston, centrally located and sometimes dubbed 'Little Istanbul' because of its numerous Turkish shops, cafes, and men-only social clubs, was a foil to the vibrant Ridley Road market, with its street stalls and micro-shops attracting members of the African, West Indian, and South Asian communities. Further south, Shoreditch and Hoxton were to become a home for the Vietnamese diaspora, as did, to some extent, the area around Mare Street. And in the northern reaches of the borough orthodox Jews and South Asian Muslims lived and shopped cheek-by-jowl. All of this in a borough with high rates of unemployment, derelict Victorian houses, abandoned cars, piles of litter, a fast-declining industrial base and, not least, the notoriously racist police based at Stoke Newington police station. Despite all this, a community spirit about Hackney defied its problems.

Perhaps Eveline and Alan ought to have the last word in their unfinished conversation. 'See me there!' Eveline exclaimed when asked what his photographs did for her poems. To which Alan, when quizzed about what Eveline's poems did for his photographs, pithily responded: 'They're the mood music.'

Peter Archard
Hackney, 1 August 2022

Poems and Photographs

TIME

Did Columbus know
Did Columbus know
That his rediscovery would be my slave society?
Did Columbus know that his so call 'New Land',
Would be my slave camp?
As he sailed in vessels three
Niña, *Pinta*, *Santa María*.

ADOLESCENCE

Too young to be a Hippy
To old to be a Punk
Well, that's when Reggae got to me,
Roots and Culture Melody,
Lyrics that inspired me,
I found my musical identity
That satisfied the youth in me.

BAD BOY

International bad boy
Original Don Gargan
24-7, 7-11, 365
Bad Boy Racism,
Are me run things,
Go tell the people,
Go tell them boys,
Say me bad, bad, bad all the time,
Guilty of a million crimes,
Look round the world my power control
The humans just do as they are told,
Guilty of murder, rape and torture,
Brutal and wild,
Kill man, woman and child.
Make you suffer, make you live in fear
And shudder, it is I who cause you to
Live in the gutter,
For me and poverty we are chums,
Lay on the pressure, you ball oppression,
Then the stress and the strain increase the pain,
Racism on your back again,
Obstacles rain, you are trying in vain,
A futureless pauper, I tie you in chains,
Prejudice on my left, Discrimination on my right,
Together we control your life.

RECESSION

That ugly beast that dare to feast,
Yes on the rich,
Which ugly teeth print bankrupt grief
Cause years of toil
To fall, infecting all,
Beyond the walls, where bugs crawl in homes unfit,
Recession reigns with no sign of defeat.

INSPIRATION

You're the best
Lyricist there is,
Jehovah God,
Guide me, guide me, guide me
Please,
Got to find the words to refresh the soul,
Of so many millions growing old,
Jehovah God,
Guide me, guide me, guide me please,
You are the best lyricist there is,
Like David of old, let my lyrics refresh the soul,
The tension and the stress the pen express,
Like David of old,
Let my lyrics refresh the soul.

INFORMATION

As a simple one,
I can understand,
That the average man
Needs a helping hand,
See the youth in the pram,
He is gonna be a man,
Need education, mansion and land,
What am I gonna say,
When he ask me, Mum,
Why few have many,
And many have none?
Why some up so,
And some down so?
Why we always sit in de same damn back row?
Why look before we leap?
Why see and blind?
Oh and why deaf and dumb?

RACISM

I am Racism
I am Racism
And I want everyone to know
That I am the most evil, wicked, bad, disgusting thing
That has ever revealed himself to you
I kill, murder, torture and imprison millions over the century,
I am the champion serial killer,
No one can equal my records for mass murders,
History tells of my conquest,
Every world power has used me
To manipulate corrupt and kill
Throughout their reign.
I am Racism, covert or overt,
I am dangerous.

ALONE

In the land of
I didn't say that
The desert flower blooms
Together with the isolated one.

I, Theodore, lay beneath the crimson sky,
And drink the warm milk from Massa's cow,
As I race across the flooded rivers of the unsolved problems,
I come across deadly shades
Of glistering red and yellows,
The golden sub-sunlight's blinding
The misery that forever lingers,
Whether it be day or night.
Deep in the shadows the cuckoo nest,
The lily blossom stands magnificent,
And the still air makes its presence known,
As it irritate the nostrils of the inexperienced one,
I, Theodore, lay beneath the crimson sky and watch the
Long years pass by, savagely injuring my soul,
As I race across the flooded rivers of the unsolved problem,
Massa is never gonna die.

DEPRESSION

Dark tube running
Indefinitely,
Dense darkness,
Is it the burden of life?
Pressure mounting,
Desires crumbling,
Soul searching,
Banging,
Hammering,
Spirit far reaching,
Dying.
So many thirsty for natural love,
Isolated,
Desolated,
Dispirited,
Society's madness,
Rough wind coming, uprooting
Defeating,
Man-made foundation and ideologies are passing,
The truth is tormenting,
The temple is cracking.

SAD

Between the mountains
Known as sorrow and grief,
Tearful waterfalls flow.

AWARENESS

Just because you feel safe
And sound,
Don't think your ground won't shake
And come down,
Bomb went off in the city street,
People running here and there,
Emergency services everywhere,
Danger, black smoke, get clear
Of flying glass, one must beware,
There is nothing deader than
What you fear,
So be alert and take care,
Keep safe is what I hear.

TRAVELLING

The roar and thunder of the
Approaching train did rattle the
Window pane,
But as it passes peace came back at last
And I open my coffee flask.
You fancy a cup, oh you would rather not,
So, I settled my head, but
Would have rather my bed,
Two hundred miles to go on the tracks,
One better find some way to relax.
The roar and thunder of the passing train did rattle
The window pane.

STREET LAW

New seas that springs,
Bears fruits of sins,
The heart of man has caved right in
To things that glitter, a diamond digger, for money,
Many pulls the trigger,
A contract killer.

JUNK UP

A rackertac rapp,
A rackertac rapp,
Every day you there in a trap,
Tell it where it's at,
There's more to life than
Crack.

THINKING

To want is but a simple thing,
To get is much harder.
Not for everyone do bells ring,
Or birds sing,
And rhythms of delight
Transform the acoustic of the soul.
If it was possible the mind boggles to think,
What has been done and what could be
Done if one tries,
To want is but a simple thing
To get is much, much harder.

FOOD

Say me hungry and me
Starving,
And you throw away de good, good grain.
Say me hungry and me starving and you tell me to
Pray for rain,
On the elements you put the blame,
But I know it's your greed for grain.
Say me hungry and me starving and I know you are
Using your brain,
There is more than enough to share with us stored,
And it is a long time before rain,
As I wait in vain.
And the needy die because of the greedy.
When one hungers for wealth,
There is no virtue or principles,
Just self-preservation.
Say me hungry and me starving.

THANKS

Only you, Jehovah, stops the
Water from going further than the shore,
Only you, Jehovah, can ever bring any
Comfort to the poor.
When I watch the flowers grow,
Or the earth covered in snow,
I know Jehovah loves forever more.

ABUSE

At a glance I saw you,
So full of youth, a bubbling pool
Of life, energetic truth,
A springy, bouncy bag of joy,
At a glance I saw you, not so young,
Like an old man your footstep pace
Got caught in the race,
Cannot look anyone in the face,
There is no place,
No one to take your case,
At a glance I saw you.

CARING FOR EACH OTHER

We all need counselling,
And we all need comforting,
But the opportunity to do the
Counselling and the comforting,
Never seems to arise,
as much as one would like.
Yet one sighs with grief
At a withered rose,
We all need counselling and
We all need comforting.

AFRICAN-CARIBBEAN WOMAN

Things are not always what they seem,
So, lift up your head and straighten your spine,
And develop your mind.
Black woman, you can motivate, inspire,
Achieve and acquire whatsoever you desire.
Don't let past history dog you
Into a state of non-existence,
Yes, don't let no one mould you
Into how society see you,
Many battles you have fought single handed,
Not forgetting the war is yet to come.
Your strength and determination are
Secretly admired globally.
Your ability to adapt to sudden change,
And survive horrendous treatment is
One that has baffled generations.
Black woman, even you can reach the
Top of the spiral staircase,
Even you can climb Mount Everest.
Building a future on respect and dignity,
Demanding it wherever you go.
Things are not always what they seem,
The price of liberty is eternal vigilance.

DOWN IN THE GHETTO

Down in the ghetto where me and
Abba grow,
That's the place that politicians never go.
They leave the dealers there to steal the show,
The rock star in the doorway burns the snow.
Those who live there have no place to go,
Down in the ghetto where me and Abba grow.
Hosanna for the love that flows,
Hosanna for the peace in the misery.

DOWN IN THE GHETTO II

Down in the ghetto where the cowboy comes from,
Contentment is something so hard to find,
Every day you wake up and say:
What you gonna do with yourself today,
But deep in your mind you know that you are only
Wasting your time
Going down to the same old Frontline.
Down in the ghetto where the cowboy comes from,
A heavy burden always clouds the mind,
Every day you wondering, wondering,
What you gonna do.
Every day you sing the same old song too.

PRAY

Rinse my soul clean of the want
For vengeance,
For I must live free, far from the
Bitterness that cripples the soul
Grinding bones and tying knots in the heart,
Causing it to get as hard as stones,
Human that I am craving better best,
But not at the expense of another soul.

LIVING

One treble, three double,
Pray master God, get me out of this trouble,
You hold on to me hand like you don't understand,
You do not fit in my plan,
No matter how much money,
No matter how much fame,
You never gonna get to use my name.
I get up every day, to Jehovah I pray,
Keep my simple mind from floating away,
With so many people confuse today,
You have to be careful what you think and say.
One treble, three double,
Pray master God, get me out of this trouble,
If there is a way point it out I pray,
One cannot trust anybody today.

59

Pinned nose and metal-pierced eyebrows
Glared, pressed against the glass,
Class, bureaucracy, plutocracy and democracy
all under attack,
Regurgitation of the hidden ugliness and rotten violence
that breeds doom,
Pale white, half-starved, modern man, pale
in his modern world,
meant to drive fear and honestly scare
all in the hope of being as far from
the norm as possible.
Pinned nose and metal-pierced eyebrows
Pressed against the glass
Broken rules, lies used as a manipulative tool,
Claiming even those who are far from being fools.

56

As I wait hanging in isolation,
Thinking how soul eat soul,
So cheap to kill,
In our modern nuclear zone,
As acid rain poured down the corn road,
The soil laid poisoned and torn from
Years of abuse,
Some say chemical misuse,
All for profit,
What a loss, a hole in the zone crust,
As I wait hanging in isolation,
Thinking on how soul eat soul,
How so cheap to kill.

Catch a 35 down a' Brixton
Man just a' go to rally round
Dilly dally round the front line
I and I feel ire inside
Down in the alley me talk to Mr Wally
Him a' kick football
Smack against the wall
Him a' chant say Babylon must fall
Man and man have to live on
Man and man can't be on the run
If you deal in violence
You must go down in silence
If you deal in violence
You don't have any sense
Catch a 35 down a' Brixton
Raving about in these dread times
Man and man have so much on his mind
Him put his head pon de line
You don't need no licence
For crime and violence
A' it dread on de line
De man them full of wine
Them a' dilly dally round the poverty line
Moving and grooving and stepping with the times
Come in, Baby, hit me with some of your nursery rhymes
Make sure it's in rhythm and time
Stepping it lightly down a' front line
Strolling on the street sweating from the heat

Meet up on a thief about to make a hit
Me ball out brother Keith
There's a thief at your hip
He move so quick he slip and miss the brick
The bitch miss the lick
Brother Keith kiss him teeth
The man them won't work and they wonder why them broke
Them sit on the line and just crack joke
Them a' dilly dally round all the time
See them there pon the line.

57

Rootless and homeless on the bench
You rest,
Drinking, bickering, chanting, cursing
The fiery souls that dare disturb your course
Of doom and destruction with words of
'Live up to reality,'
'Better to be dry,'
As the bitterness twist and tear your soul
The tin can held tight,
Watches the lip for another swallow.
Rootless and homeless on the bench you rest,
Blocking out yesterday, today and thoughts of tomorrow.

58

Waiting for the voice I long to hear,
Really, really clear a chance to meet in privacy,
Communicating openly,
Holding tight the opportunity to build friendship,
Leading to relationship plain for the world to see,
Waiting, waiting for the voice to meet,
Put together whole and complete,
Take the chance to jump and skip.

60A

Invisible chains of control repress
Your soul,
You hold close to your breast
Your secret that must never be told,
The desire for someone to trust unfolds,
To wake up and find that it was but a dream.
To plan and succeed in a getaway beam,
Yet caged you be by the power that surround thee.
How can you be free when there is no need?
For a model prisoner, invisible chain of control represses
Your soul.

60B

The need to be free seem to be bursting out of thee,
Sitting on the highest cloud,
The envy of millions all about, each one would give their soul
To swap places with you there,
But your reality is not what they feel and see,
They would be shock if the truth was told enough,
Bearing up is carrying ten thousand cross,
Doing well is living in their hypocritical hell,
The image and the hope,
Reputation must keep high,
If you want to be one of the few that survive,
Close doors close ranks and into disassociation plunge.
The need to be free seems to be bursting out of thee.

47

The moon up there
High in the sky, so bright,
Looking at you and I

***

I want to resurrect your love,
Like a phoenix from the ashes,
Let it rise rekindled,
Red hot ladder running deep into my soul
Spread your wings and fly,
Now refuelled with passion.

***

Dem de, de girl
Who lick the crack pipe,
Selling your body for a stone every night,
Hustling, gambling, the price is your life,
Making your mother hold her head and asking God why,
Tried so hard to provide, made 'nough sacrifice,
So you can have a good life.

Write about woman . . . you say,
Black woman . . .
write about me . . .
Black woman catapulted globally . . .
Mashed like grated manioc . . .
Worn out like khaki beaten on river stones,
Like carefully washed clothes spread out on wild bushes . . .
She dries . . .
But does not wither,
From eight 'till four on the factory floor . . .
£1.20 an hour, even her youngest son earns much much more.

***

Am looking forward to the life
'Ave yet to know
Contentment is a special seed to sow,
As you live you get to know
Love is a precious grain to grow.

BLACK WOMAN

Despite your history and your legacy,
You blossom,
You spread your seeds across the sea.
You deserve an accolade, a just reward
Precious may it be.
So bold, so brave, such courage
I salute your sincerity,
Living in this treacherous society with its forest
Of atrocities.
You have reached the peaks that your forefathers
Would never see,
You have crossed the bridge in centuries gone,
No feet your shade dare touch the ground
In leaps and bounds you progress on
Teaching your offspring knowledge that is sound.
Such might and strength to battle on,
Conscious of the fears that lurks in and around,
Despite the derogatory terms they pick,
The names and labels do not stick.
Your critics have to bite their lips, as their
Assumptions crumble and their ideologies tumble,
You stand victorious on your feet.
Although your wings they clip,
You rise above the dirt they heap,
Your dignity you get to keep.
If opportunities are few and far between,
Then the wind of change still carries

The masters reign,
When the snares of oppression rains acid pain,
You tie your waist, look your offspring in the face
And pray that life tolls they can control,
At the bottom of the food chain,
You who plant the seeds and grains,
The harvest others reap, to store in heaps and heaps,
Keeping cost beyond your reach,
The dirtiest work that they could find,
The lowest wage across the times,
The brutal condition was so unkind,
The memories blocked out of your mind,
The poverty of yesterday you pray that tomorrow never brings,
As you watch them plot and scheme
To destroy your children's dream.
It's a global thing,
The fears of millions of unwanted kin,
Brings an uneasy feeling within,
Knowing how the system thinks,
Now your voice in the chambers of power,
Climbing the confidence ladder,
Winning opportunities, opening doors and
Challenging laws,
We are celebrating a new beginning,
The birth of a new century coming in, imagine a hundred years
Of history in a flash,
Despite your history and your legacy,
You blossom, flower and
Spread your seeds across the sea.

THE MAZE

I see the young man walking the street,
Hands stretched deep in empty pockets,
An expressionless face relates his
Disposition caused by confusion.
He wears his hat out of tradition
Sheltering his head,
Not from the sun, but from the cold.
Oh why, oh why does he step without meaning?
Nowhere to go to,
Nowhere to go back to.
Who is to blame?
He blames himself, oh no, not his race.
He kicks his heels in the dirty street,
And gets another slap on the cheek,
Self-inflicted of course,
Trying to slap away his worry and stress.
He remembers the days,
Oh yes, how could he forget?
When he played in the streets of Jamaica.
At least he was free,
Free with the sun,
And his mother carried the burden and stress,
He prayed, Oh Lord he prayed,
For a life without tension, aggravation
And stress.
A life without sorrow
And with a meaningful step,
Oh why can't he be like storybook children?
He remembers in time that the true lesson
Of life
Is how much can you take without being a fake.

The day the African came
Nothing seem to be the same
The day the African came
Gran Ma was deep in her cocoa trees
I was busy feeding the hens
Brother Tootoo was chopping wood under the
Star-apple growth whilst Old Faithful
Doze in the late afternoon sun.
And there was the African coming towards me
Head bent, deep in thought, wrapped in foreign cloth
The radiant rays of light dance through the
Leaves high up over the trees
Creating an air so unexplainable
Just like the African
Engrossed in what seemed to be an immensity of thought
The African was quite unaware of Old Faithful
Running towards him full of aggression
I stepped in at that moment and seized Faithful
And there I was face to face with a real live African.
In books I read of him
In magazines I gazed at portraits of him
Yes, it's really 'him', the African from the
Land I did know, and didn't know
However will get to know again
Gran Ma, brother Tootoo, come make haste
The unexpected guest has arrived
Bon après-midi, mademoiselle
Good afternoon, young lady, his voice echoed
Through my mind,
An Anglo-French speaking African
An African speaks African
Gran Ma and brother Tootoo stepped in and made up for
My manners, setting before the African a feast.
I stared and stared, glancing across to the mirror
I looked at myself, then to Gran Ma and brother Tootoo
And back to the African.

World economic crisis chaos on the streets
The masses are marching against the government that they pick,
The young generation look on in vain,
Their elders can no longer convince them there's something to gain.
Who's going to take the blame when the riots start again?
World economic crisis chaos on the streets
Poverty is on the beat, job creation has fallen down the pit.
Who's going to represent the jobless, the
Homeless and those who just walk the streets?
Is there hope for the futureless children
who can't compete with the microchip?
Politicians, social workers and those who are concerned
all claim to represent the poverty-stricken
souls from days of old when they gave out
soup bowls.
A promise is a comfort to a fool.
They're only using you as a tool,
An instrument to fulfil their own ambitions.
Look there's one suffering from malnutrition
Help him, expect nothing,
Then you won't be disappointed when you receive nothing.

It is not for you to ask the question why,
But for you to follow instruction and dispel the lie,
There is no pot of gold at the end of the rainbow,
No one guarantees you blue sky,
Youth man be wise
Do not believe traditional lies,
That makes a very complicated life,
It is impossible for God to lie,
Man will work hard for his living,
And by the sweat of their brow he shall eat,
So, find work and get off the street.
Don't bother take up the concept of those who
Go to bed with 'I want' and get up with 'Give me'
And 'Lend me a money',
As for the get-rich-quick clique,
With their cons, tricks and fast money chicks.
Youth man get wise, one needs to organise one's self
Now more than ever before,
Youth man articulate yourself, make good use of the opportune time,
Hold fast to what is fine,
Liberate your mind, every one of us has the ability to overcome
Any pressure or stress we encounter,
Discover your inner strength and build your relationship
With the most high
It is not for you to ask the question why,
But for you to dispel the lie.
There is so many choosing to fashion themselves on the system,
Mimicking the host society,
Partaking in low life and debauchery
As sorry souls, they fall by the wayside,
Tormented by a discontented life.
Youth man, when you wake up and open your eyes,
Think truthfully, think thoughtfully and think thoroughly
You could achieve whatever you desire,
Hard work will ensure your success.

Youth man, do not follow those who brag and boast,
About they run things and things don't run them.
The system has the strategy, the powers-that-be has
A surprise for thee,
Oh youth man, there are many who would try to mislead you
And make you fall in the bottomless pit.
Jehovah has made his provision to guide us out of the hole and creek.
The sacred book is worth more than the food we need to eat.

CARE

Why can't we be good to each other,
No need to fear or even shudder,
Don't we know we need each other
For this, that, or whatever.

AFRICAN QUEEN

She is beauty in appearance,
Cool, calm and collected in a crisis,
Most elegant in dress
And classy in style,
Deep, dark in complexion,
Pretty like a raven in flight,
Cool and courageous like a lioness,
Mystery and intense fantasy,
Overpower my beautiful raven,
She is troubled, she's imprisoned
In her thoughts,
Tragedy and pain is embedded in
Her subconscious mind,
She is strong, she is agile,
She will survive,
She fights day and night,
She is not alone,
The light of my father shines bright,
On my beautiful raven,
Forever and ever she shall survive,
My African queen.

DAMN ADAM

I no longer welcome the morning sun.
Damn Adam
As I pull on the big head and know
I have admitted defeat,
Escapism is not freedom,
Yet every tub has its own bottom,
And the girl sat sucking her thumb,
A victim of circumstance,
Who is to tell the end of the inexperienced one?
Damn Adam
When immorality has taken over and sensual
Pleasure has been misrepresented as an act of love
And the truth they cannot see,
Or hear,
Or feel, and this illusion they call reality.
Damn Adam
Locked in the claws of everyday routine
Of doing 'nothing', one seems to slowly drift away,
Needless to say a disappointed soul.
Damn Adam
Say it again, Damn Adam,
From morning till night, no comfort for you, oh
Miserable man,
Where is your strength?
Your might? You always boast of how you can fight
But
When the fight is with yourself,
You just give up like a worm, you
Yes you
Damn Adam, say it if it makes you feel better.
Damn Adam
I no longer welcome the morning sun.

In my name and interest
I demand answers to countless questions.
Why oh why
Am I over-represented in every correctional and penal system?
In whose interest, has
Countless research and analysis been conducted,
And to what end?
Yet you know nothing about me,
From global perspective you gather information,
Who knows the secrets about me?
However, you don't feel you know enough about
How I think, to ascertain as to how to help me.
In my name and in my interest,
I demand answers to countless questions,
What's so interesting about the black man?
Yet still more research,
Why do you fear the black man?
Powerless, no army, no money,
With the burden of the legacy of slavery,
The powers that be inject him with diseases,
The powers that be contaminate his blood,
The powers that be try and kill him with man-made
Famines and countless wars.
In my name and in whose interest.

Seas upon seas of
Countless crowds,
Moving, stopping, watching,
In merriment of joy,
Sounds of laughter,
Sounds of musical power,
To the first timer, unbelievable,
Out of this world,
Seas upon seas of countless crowds
Seduced by the mystic CARNIVAL CLOUD.

VIBES

Feel the carnival spirit when the
Music hits,
From street-to-street dancing to a variety of beats
Taste the culture
Taste the custom
Rich and alive is the spirit on carnival night
Inspiring, reinforcing, strengthening,
Confidence in numbers
Feel the carnival spirit when the
Music hits.

SOCIAL CHANGE

Everyone wants social change,
but you won't get it
playing chess
taking drugs
hanging around in coffee bars
making excuses
moaning
moping.
Everyone wants social change,
but you won't get it
blaming everything and anyone except yourself
taking up photography
arts and crafts
painting video making.
Everyone wants social change,
up and down the country there are many sitting around
waiting
wanting
forever wishing that someone, somewhere, will bring about
change.
Looking from the gutter up, one sees clear to the top.
Equality is not freedom.

LET'S MAKE HISTORY

So we know about slavery
We write about it
We sing about it
So we know about slavery, so we unearth our history
Alright . . . what next?
When do we draw the line and say, to the best of our ability,
Come, let's make modern history . . .

p. 2 **Stoke Newington High Street, 1979**. The Stoke Newington town guide had seen better days. It used to display a map of the area and if you pressed the buttons you could light up the location of various shops and services on the map, a technological marvel that was very popular with children.

pp. 6-7 **Ridley Road, 1979**. Kossoff's all-night bagel shop attracted a strange mix of black-cab drivers, random inebriates and spaced-out party people.

p. 9 **Finsbury Park, 1975**. I shared a flat in a slum on the Common with Babs Fawehinmi, and sometimes he'd borrow my camera and take it out on his rounds. He took this photo of his mates playing football on a warm summer's day in Finsbury Park.

p. 10 **TV news, 1983**. The news media were always happy to give airtime to Enoch Powell, one of the Tories' top racists.

p. 12 **Hackney Town Hall, 1980**. May Day march against Thatcherism.

p. 15 **Sandringham Road**. The Greater London Council (GLC) even protected our temporary open spaces for us.

pp. 16-18 **Stoke Newington police station, 1979**. Michael Ferreira was a young Black man who died after he was stabbed in a fight with white racists. He went to Stoke Newington police station for help, but they delayed calling an ambulance and he bled to death there.

Two local teenagers got five years in prison for Michael's manslaughter. His funeral procession went right past the station. Ferreira wasn't the first Black person to die after contact with officers from Stoke Newington police station: that was Aseta Simms in 1972. After Michael's death, there was Colin Roach in 1983, Oluwashijibomi 'Shiji' Lapite in 1994 and Rashan Charles in 2017.

p. 21 **Andre Street, 1978**. A quiet Sunday afternoon, the workshops under the railway arches lie silent.

p. 22 **Brooke Road, 1984**. The notorious 'bums' poster. When the Tories set out to undermine Labour councils by cutting their funding, Hackney Council and local people responded with meetings, leaflets, protest marches and petitions. This Hackney Council poster against the cuts was condemned in the local press for being obscene, another example of what the tabloids called the 'Loony Left' at work. Bums weren't enough though: the cuts happened and local democracy ebbed away.

p. 24 **Mare Street, 1984**. Turkish workers and local trade unions demonstrate against racist Tory immigration laws. This was just after the arbitrary deportation of a local Turkish family, the Hasbudaks, in April 1984.

p. 25 **Graham Road, 1984**. If Margaret Thatcher, the Tory Prime Minister, felt able to tell us on TV that, 'People are rather afraid that this country might be swamped by people with a different culture,' it was no surprise that immigration officials and the Tory media were stepping up their campaign against so-called 'illegal aliens'.

p. 27 **Downs Park Road, 1978.** Walls, bus shelters, shop windows, lamp-posts, hoardings, buses and on the tube . . . everywhere you looked you'd see racist National Front graffiti, stickers, leaflets and posters. Anti-fascists painted over the graffiti and put up their own anti-fascist slogans, which would then attract more NF daubings . . .

p. 28 **Stoke Newington Road, 1984.** The Tories and their friends in the media hated the Labour-controlled Greater London Council because it was implementing radical strategies like the London-wide introduction of anti-racist and anti-sexist policies. This poster records a poll of Londoners showing strong support for the GLC . . . all to no avail: in 1986 the Tories abolished it.

p. 33 **Clissold Park, 1981.** On the day of Charles and Diana's wedding, Stoke Newington Anti-Nazi League laid on a musical alternative to the fawning sycophancy of the TV spectacular: 'Funk the Wedding'!

p. 34 **Winchester Place, 1984.** Ridley Road Market overspill on Winchester Place.

p. 36 **Sandringham Road, 1983.** The 'Frontline' on Sandringham Road was where young Black men met to socialise and where they were regularly harassed by the police; it could get a bit rowdy. It was an open secret that the local drug trade was controlled by the

violent racists from Stoke Newington police station and, if anyone dared to get in their way, they paid a heavy price.

p. 40 **Stoke Newington High Street, 1983.** Men's talk on the High Street.

p. 41 **Dalston Lane, 1984.** The Four Aces: reggae central on Dalston Lane.

p. 44 **Winchester Place, 1983.** Street drinkers.

p. 47 **Marton Road, 1984.** A 'save the GLC' poster and, beneath it, Hackney Council's response to critics of its earlier 'bums' poster (see note to p. 22).

p. 49 **Boleyn Road, 1980.** Derelict public baths.

p. 50 **Ridley Road, 1982.** Ridley Road shoppers.

p. 51 **Stoke Newington Common, 1979.** Inflation was 15 per cent, the Labour government had frozen pay rises to 5 per cent and, like a lot of other workers, the binmen went on strike for more. The rubbish piled up until they got an 11 per cent pay rise.

p. 53 **Kingsland High Street, 1980.** Waiting for the lights to change at Shacklewell Lane.

p. 54 **Dalston Lane 1983.** Waiting for the bus.

p. 55 **Stoke Newington High Street, 1979.** Mourners at Michael Ferreira's funeral.

p. 58 **Station Place, 1978.** Keeping an eye on the skinheads at Finsbury Park Carnival.

p. 60 **Stoke Newington Road, 1983.** Young man heading for Stamford Hill.

THANK YOU

Tamara Stoll for getting us to the first draft.

Junior, Monique and Sacha at Junior's for our book-meeting take-outs.

Max Leonard for his generously given help, expertise and guidance.

Myfanwy Vernon-Hunt for her generous help with design and layout.

Jenny Mules for help with editing and running the Kickstarter.

Peter Archard for contributing to our book meetings and for writing the introduction.

Lorna Gee for making time to record Eveline's poems.

INDEX OF FIRST LINES

51°33′26″N

0°04′44″W

**First published in November 2023
by Isola Press, London.
IsolaPress.com**

Images © Alan Denney
Poems © Eveline Marius
Introduction © Peter Archard

The moral right of the authors has been asserted.

Design: Myfanwy Vernon-Hunt
This-side.co.uk

Printed by Gomer Press, Wales

ISBNs: 978-1-7391267-4-2

A catalogue record for this book is available from
the British Library.

Front cover photo: see note to p. 12.
Back cover photo: see note to p. 79.